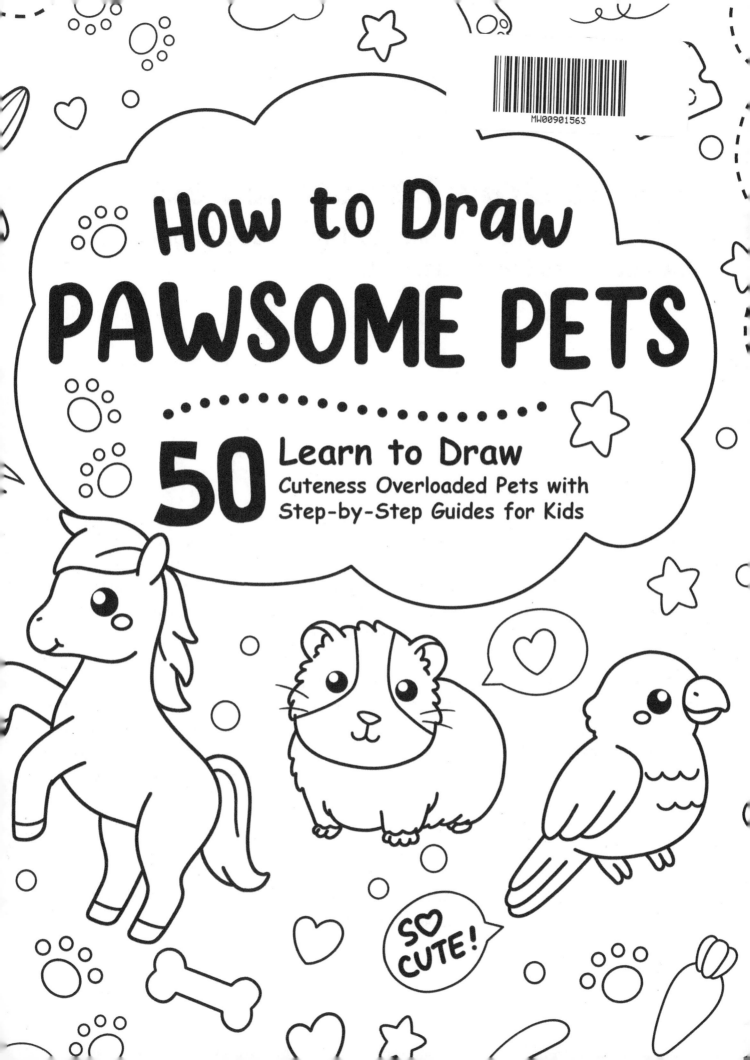

How to Draw
PAWSOME PETS

50 Learn to Draw
Cuteness Overloaded Pets with
Step-by-Step Guides for Kids

So CUTE!

How to Draw Pawsome Pets

Step-by-Step Guide for Kids to Draw Cats, Puppies, Birds and Many Cuteness-Overloaded Pets.

This Book Belongs to

TABLE OF CONTENTS

DRAWING TOOLS

Get ready to create some amazing artwork with just a few simple tools!

The pencil is your magic wand that lets you draw whatever you imagine. Different pencils have different levels of softness and hardness. Experiment with different types to find one that you like best.

If you're feeling colorful, grab some coloring materials like crayons, markers, or colored pencils to add some pop to your pictures.

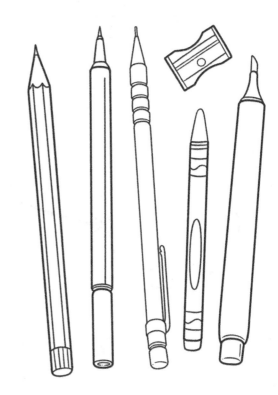

Don't forget about the trusty eraser - it's your secret weapon for fixing mistakes and making your drawings even better.

And last but not least, make sure you have a piece of paper to draw on - the possibilities are endless!

With these tools in hand, you're ready to unleash your imagination and bring your drawings to life.

BEFORE YOU START

Let's talk about the black lines and gray lines in our

1
Black lines are the start of each step in your drawing adventure!

2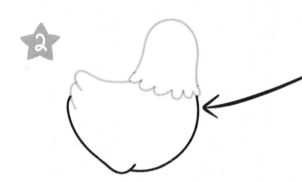
Black lines are also the new lines that you get to add to your drawing in the next steps.

3
Grey lines are the lines you've already drawn in previous steps.

4
If you come across a broken line in a step, that's a signal for you to grab your eraser and make it disappear from your drawing.

Remember, the most important thing is to have fun and enjoy the process! Keep practicing and you'll be creating amazing drawings in no time!

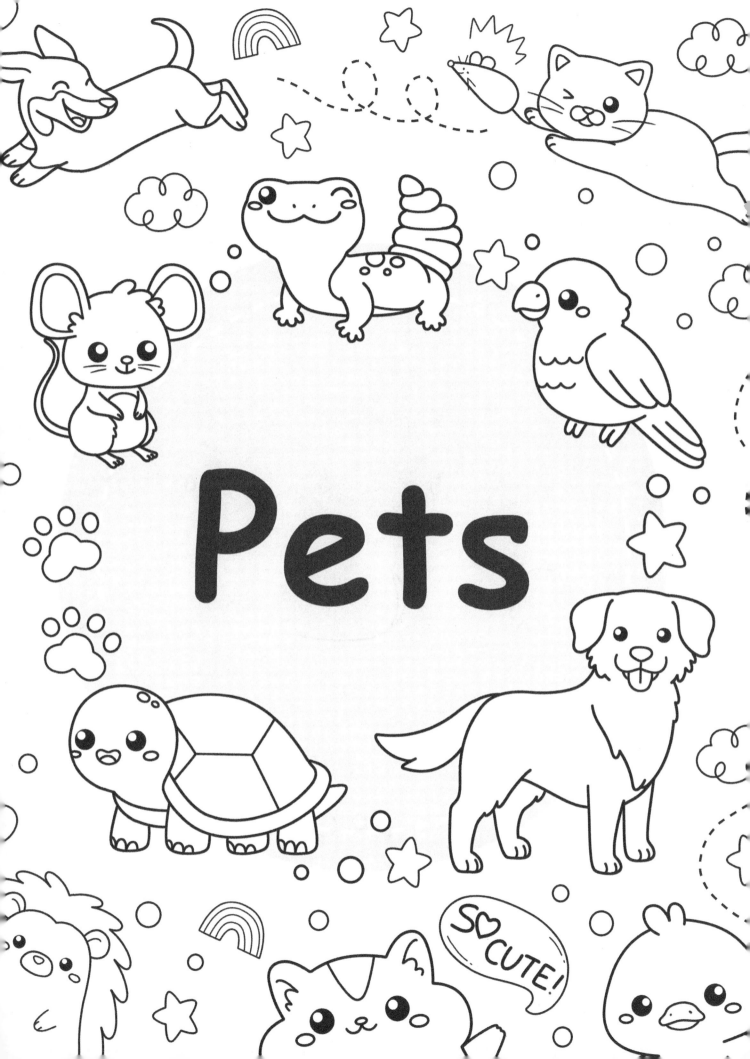

Cockatiel

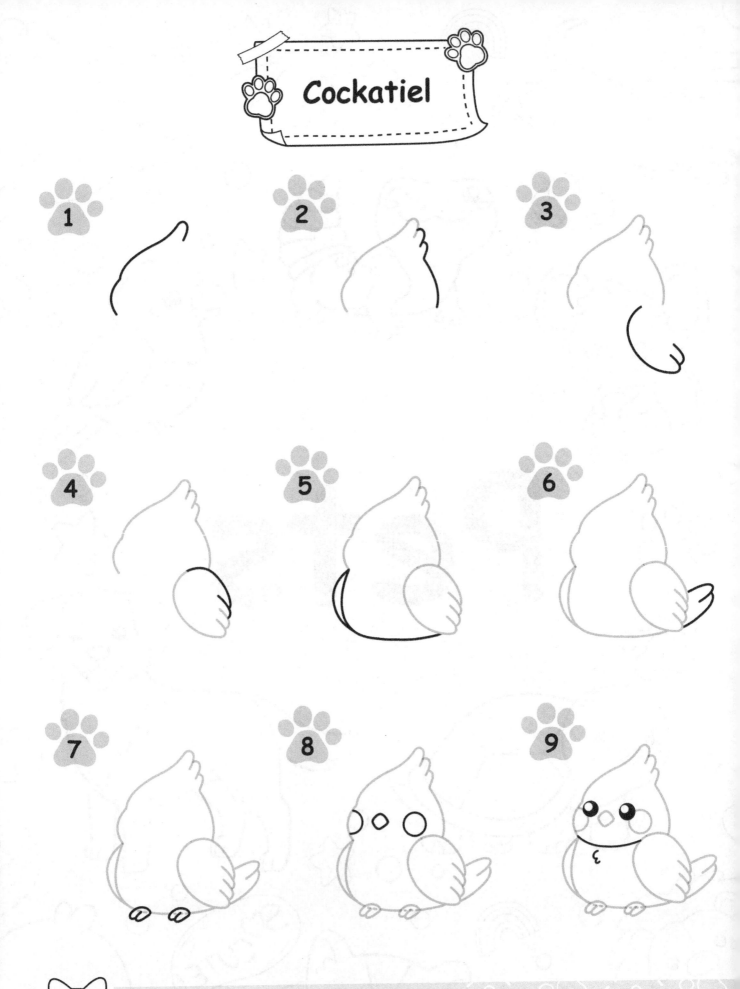

Let me be your guide,
trace and improve.

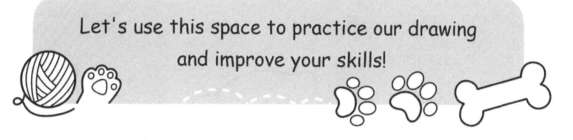

Let's use this space to practice our drawing
and improve your skills!

Sugar Glider

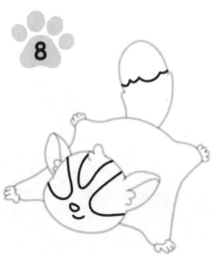

10 Sugar Glider

Follow my lines and
bring me to life!

Let's get your pencils ready and
practice drawing at this spot!

Guinea Pig

1

2

3

4

5

6

7

8

9

Trace my lines to sharpen your skills.

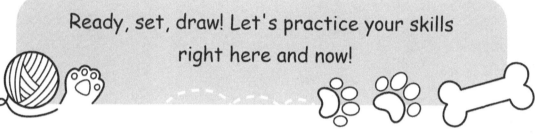

Ready, set, draw! Let's practice your skills right here and now!

Siamese Cat

Follow my outline for
a tracing challenge.

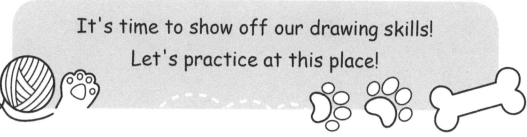

It's time to show off our drawing skills!
Let's practice at this place!

Goose

1

2

3

4

5

6

7

8

9

Hone your skills with
a trace of me.

Ready to have some fun and practice drawing?
Let's do it here!

Clownfish

Let me be your guide,
trace and improve.

Get your pencils ready,
it's time to practice drawing here!

Scorpion

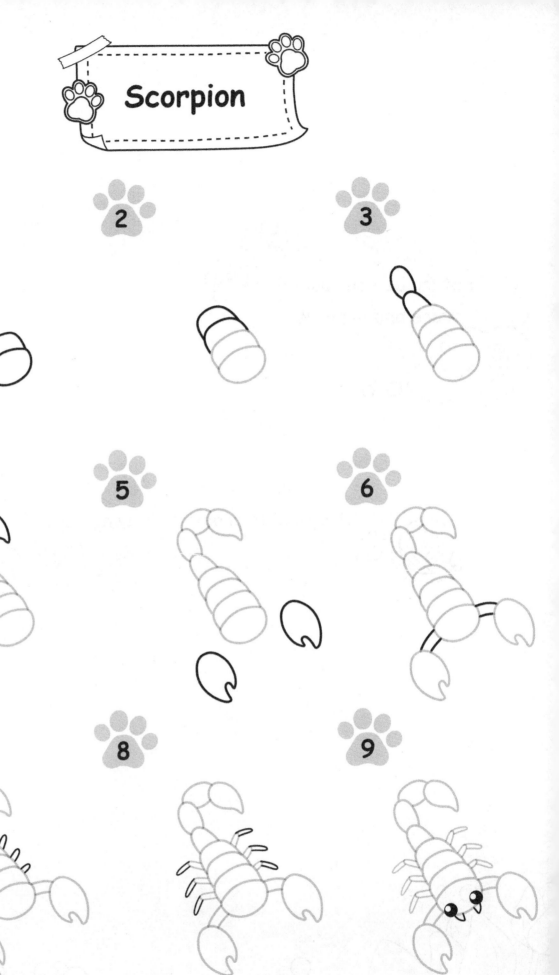

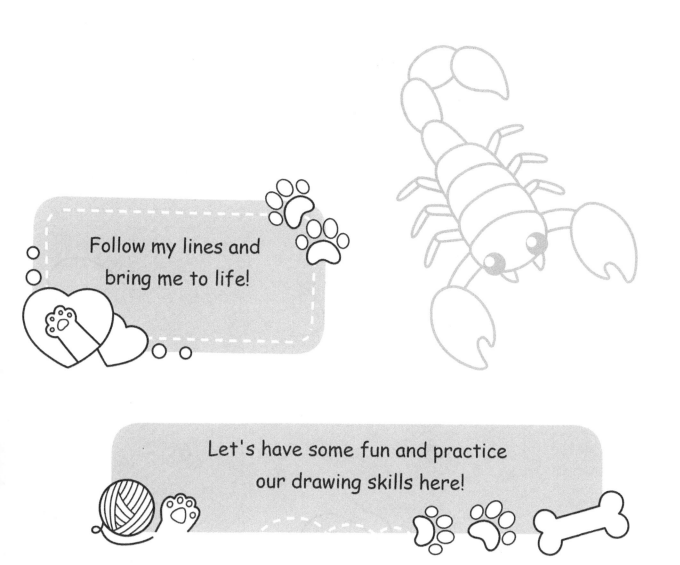

Follow my lines and
bring me to life!

Let's have some fun and practice
our drawing skills here!

Kingsnake

 1

 2

 3

 4

 5

 6

 7

 8

 9

Trace my lines to
sharpen your skills.

Are you ready to improve your drawing?
Let's practice right here!

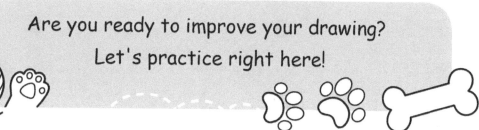

Monitor Lizard

 1

 2

 3

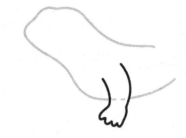

 4

 5

 6

 7

 8

 9

Follow my outline for
a tracing challenge.

Let's use this space to practice our drawing
and improve your skills!

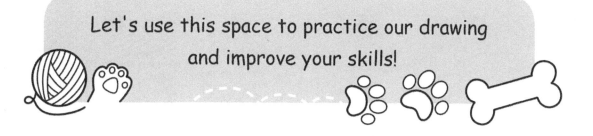

Canary

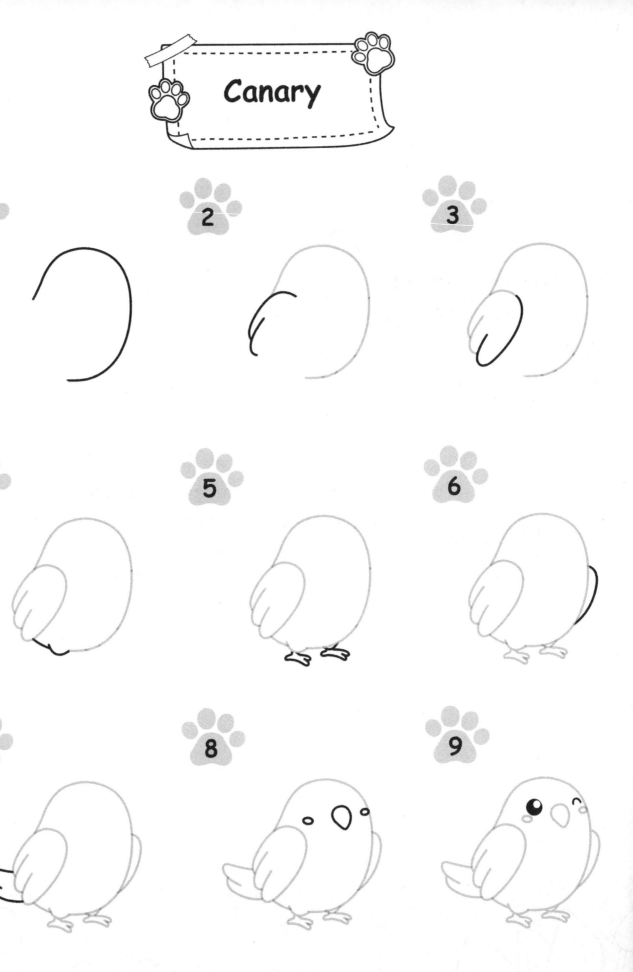

Hone your skills with
a trace of me.

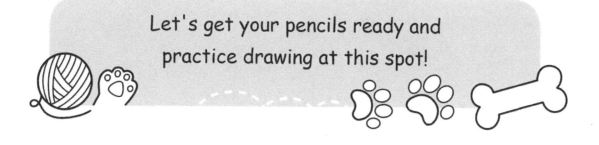

Let's get your pencils ready and
practice drawing at this spot!

Ball Python

Let me be your guide,
trace and improve.

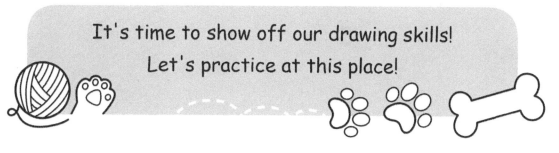

It's time to show off our drawing skills!
Let's practice at this place!

Lizard

Follow my lines and bring me to life!

Ready to have some fun and practice drawing?
Let's do it here!

Bulldog

Trace my lines to sharpen your skills.

Let's have some fun and practice our drawing skills here!

Turtle

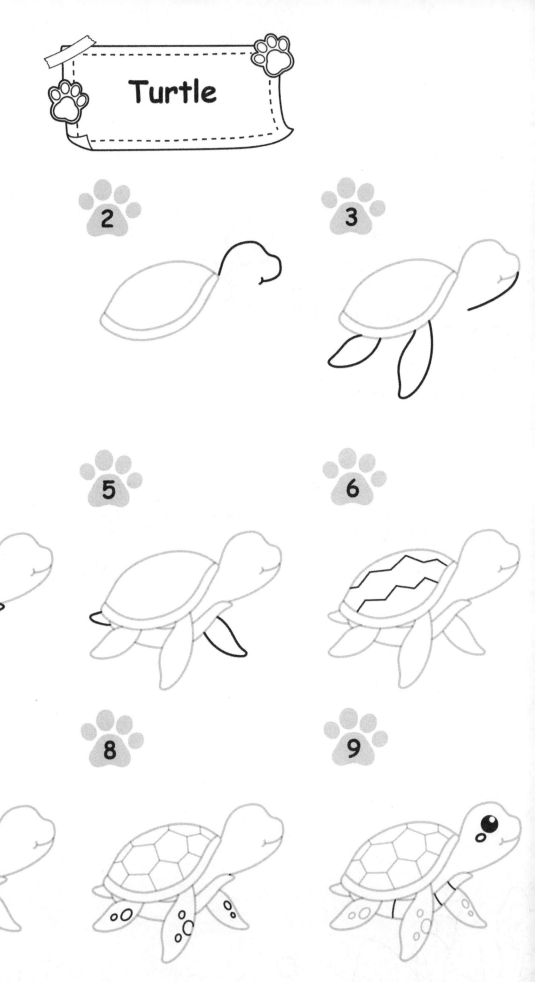

Follow my outline for a tracing challenge.

Are you ready to improve your drawing?
Let's practice right here!

German Shepherd

1

2

3

4

5

6

7

8

9

Hone your skills with
a trace of me.

Let's use this space to practice our drawing
and improve your skills!

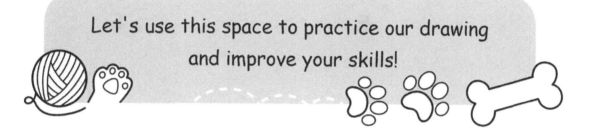

Hermit
Crab

1

2

3

4

5

6

7

8

9

38 Hermit Crab

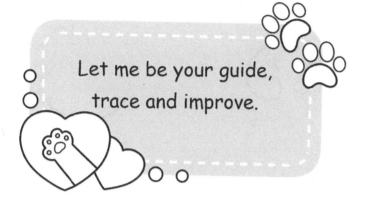

Let me be your guide,
trace and improve.

Let's get your pencils ready and
practice drawing at this spot!

Bichon

Follow my lines and
bring me to life!

Let's get your pencils ready and
practice drawing at this spot!

Betta Fish

Trace my lines to sharpen your skills.

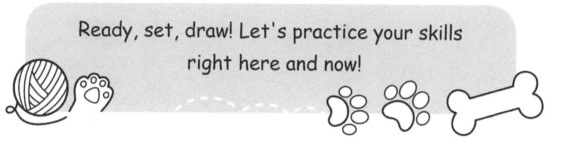

Ready, set, draw! Let's practice your skills right here and now!

Beagle

Follow my outline for a tracing challenge.

It's time to show off our drawing skills!
Let's practice at this place!

Spider

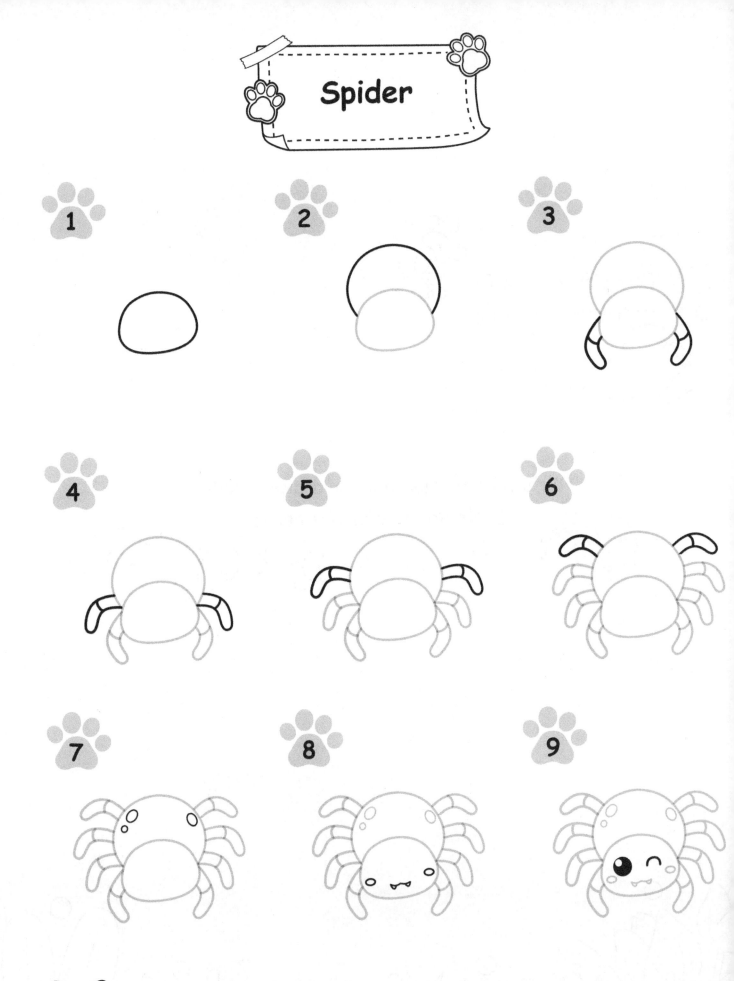

Hone your skills with
a trace of me.

Ready to have some fun and practice drawing?
Let's do it here!

Dachshund

 1

 2

 3

 4

 5

 **6**

 7

 8

 9

Let me be your guide,
trace and improve.

Get your pencils ready,
it's time to practice drawing here!

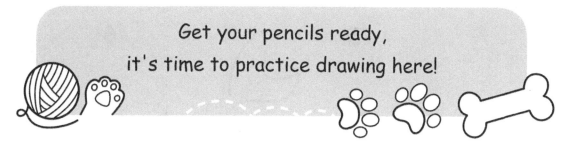

Koi

Follow my lines and bring me to life!

Let's get your pencils ready and practice drawing at this spot!

Horse

1

2

3

4

5

6

7

8

9

Trace my lines to sharpen your skills.

Let's have some fun and practice our drawing skills here!

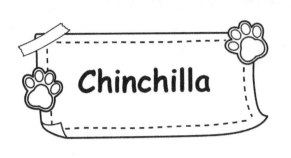

Chinchilla

1

2

3

4

5

6

7

8

9

Follow my outline for
a tracing challenge.

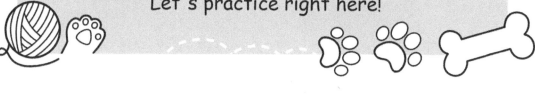

Are you ready to improve your drawing?
Let's practice right here!

Iguana

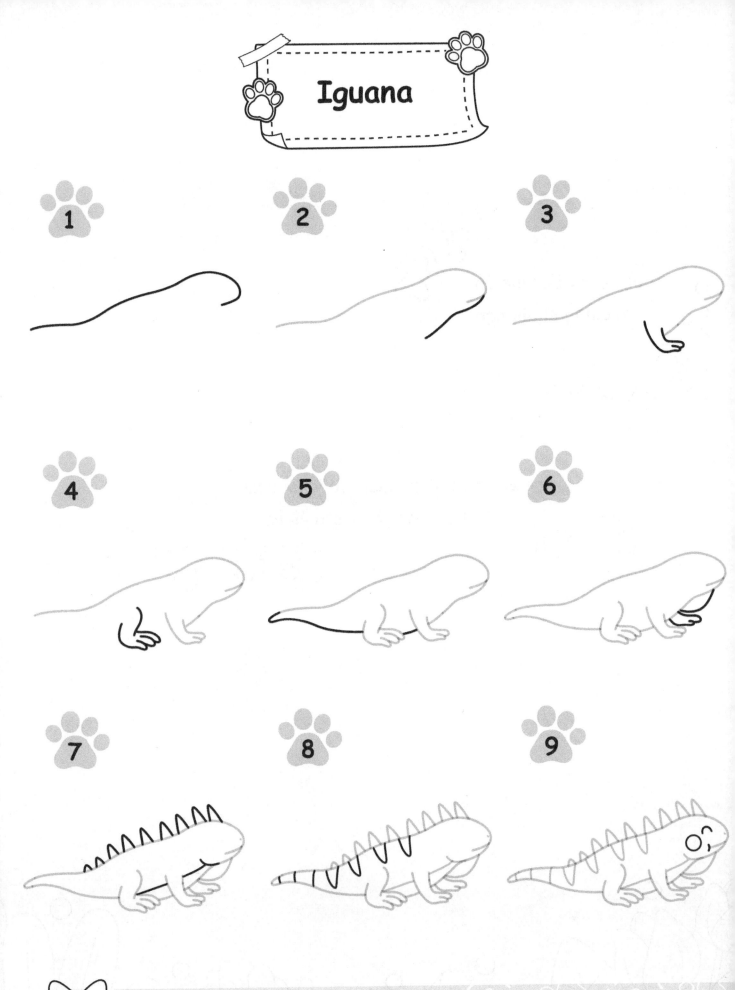

Hone your skills with
a trace of me.

Let's use this space to practice our drawing
and improve your skills!

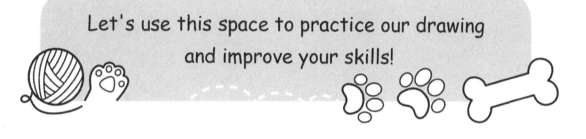

Gecko

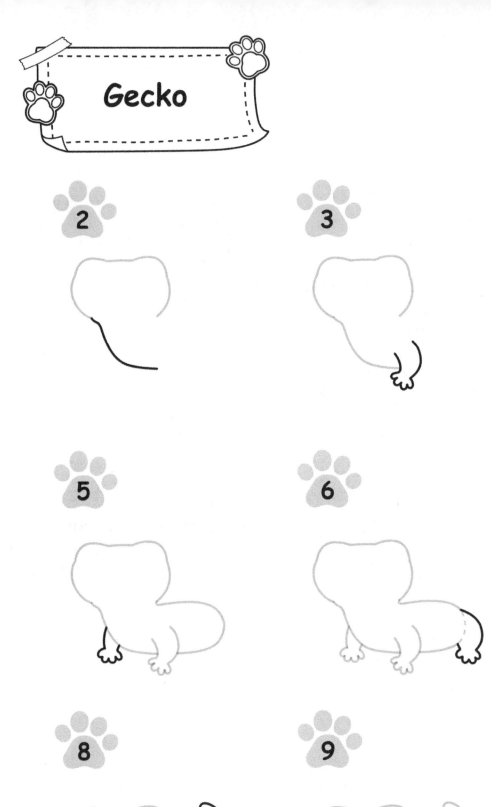

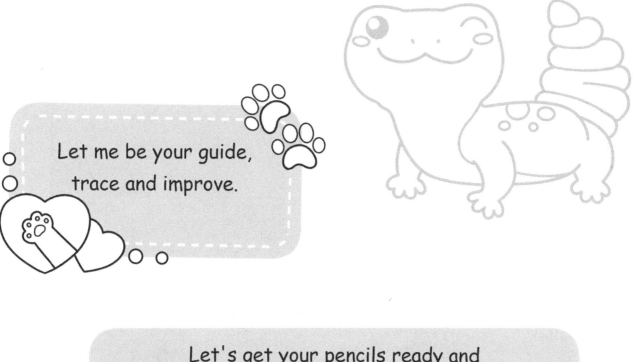

Let me be your guide,
trace and improve.

Let's get your pencils ready and
practice drawing at this spot!

Corgi

Follow my lines and
bring me to life!

Ready, set, draw! Let's practice your skills
right here and now!

Chihuahua

Trace my lines to sharpen your skills.

It's time to show off our drawing skills!
Let's practice at this place!

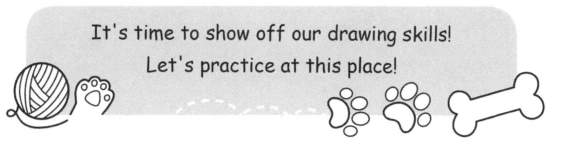

Hamster

Follow my outline for a tracing challenge.

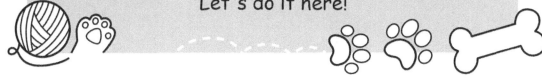

Ready to have some fun and practice drawing?
Let's do it here!

Chicken

1

2

3

4

5

6

7

8

9

Hone your skills with a trace of me.

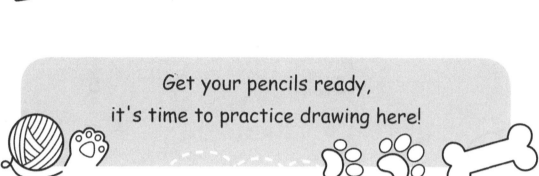

Get your pencils ready,
it's time to practice drawing here!

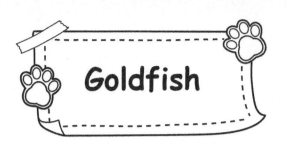

Goldfish

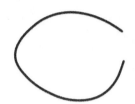

Let me be your guide, trace and improve.

Let's have some fun and practice our drawing skills here!

Parrot

Follow my lines and bring me to life!

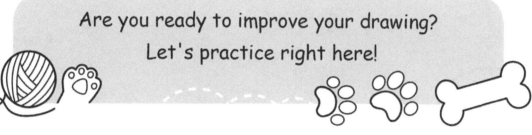

Are you ready to improve your drawing?
Let's practice right here!

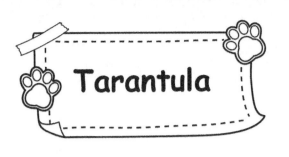

Tarantula

1

2

3

4

5

6

7

8

9

Hone your skills with
a trace of me.

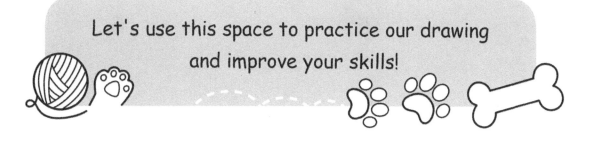

Let's use this space to practice our drawing
and improve your skills!

Ragdoll

Trace my lines to sharpen your skills.

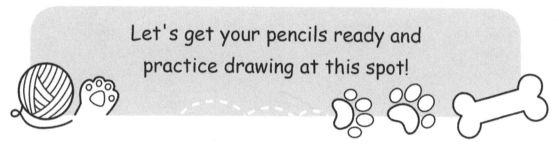

Let's get your pencils ready and practice drawing at this spot!

Frog

1

2

3

4

5

6

7

8

9

Follow my outline for
a tracing challenge.

Ready, set, draw! Let's practice your skills
right here and now!

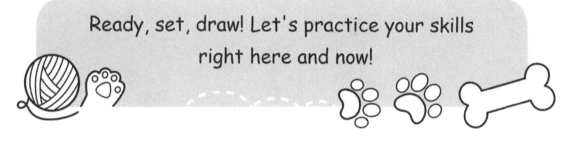

Shrimp

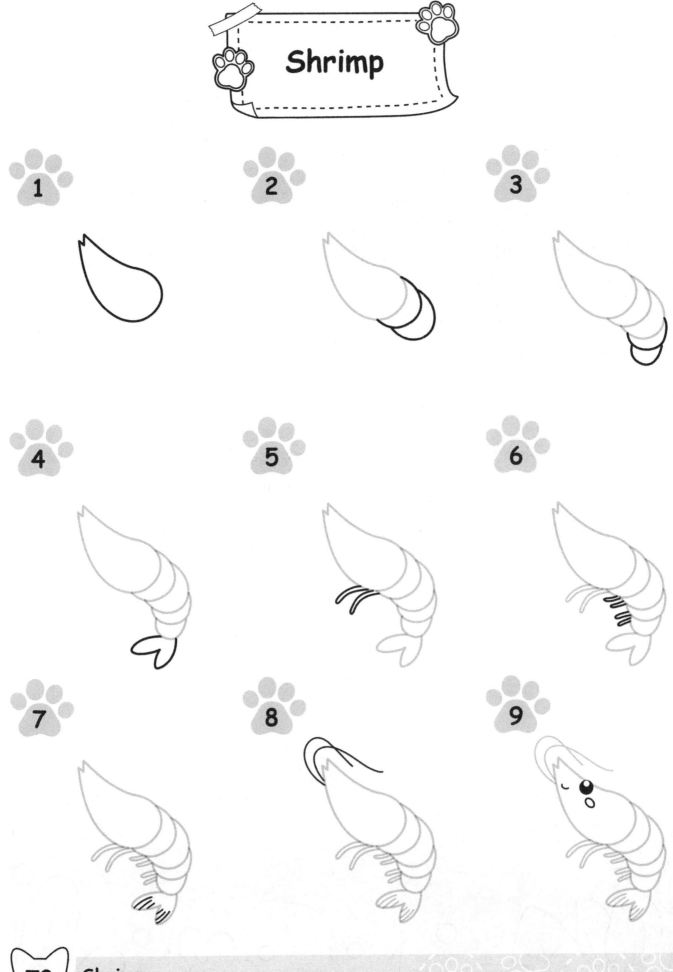

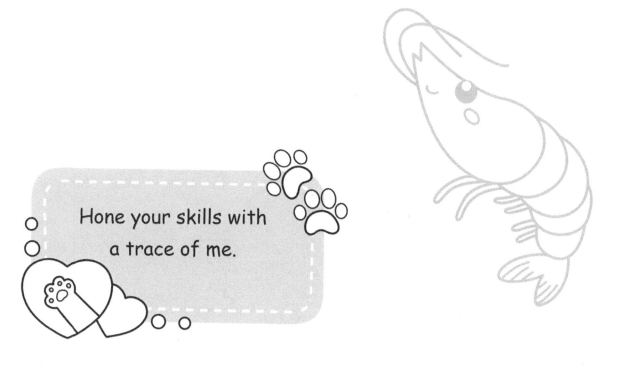

Hone your skills with
a trace of me.

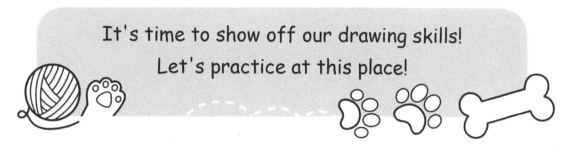

It's time to show off our drawing skills!
Let's practice at this place!

Shorthair Cat

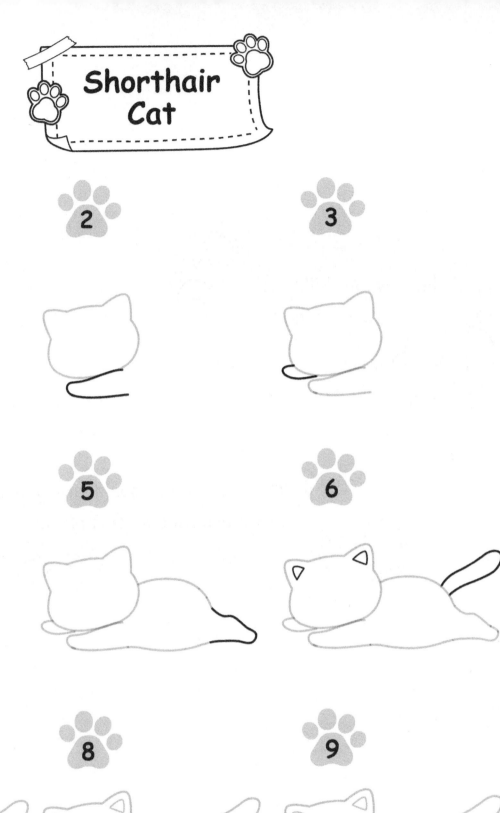

1

2

3

4

5

6

7

8

9

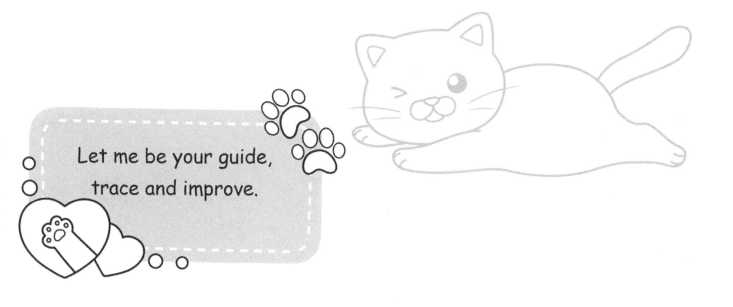

Let me be your guide, trace and improve.

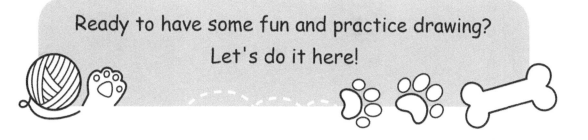

Ready to have some fun and practice drawing?
Let's do it here!

Guppy

Follow my lines and bring me to life!

Get your pencils ready, it's time to practice drawing here!

Mouse

Trace my lines to sharpen your skills.

Let's have some fun and practice
our drawing skills here!

Bearded Dragon

Follow my outline for a tracing challenge.

Are you ready to improve your drawing?
Let's practice right here!

Macaw

Hone your skills with
a trace of me.

Let's use this space to practice our drawing
and improve your skills!

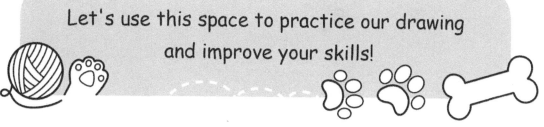

Tortoise

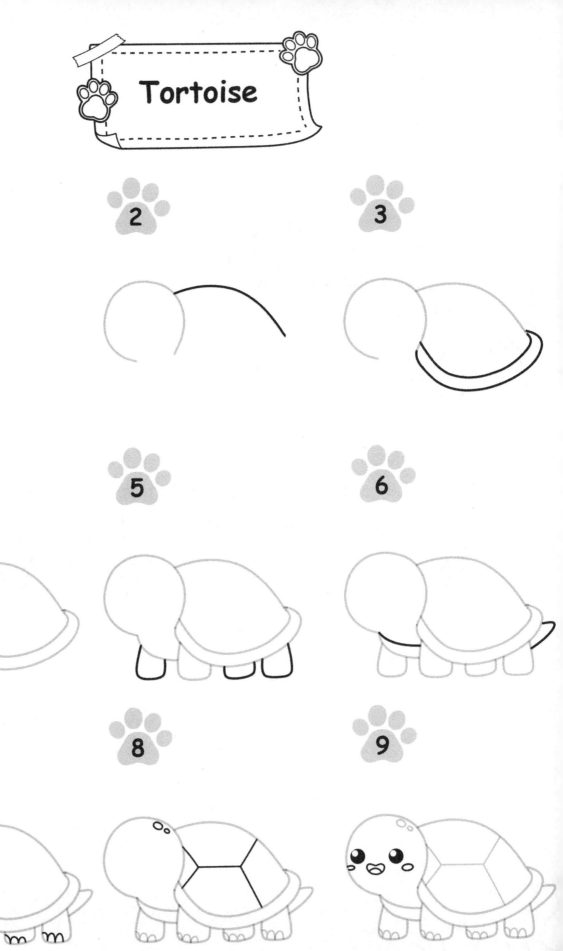

Let me be your guide,
trace and improve.

Let's get your pencils ready and
practice drawing at this spot!

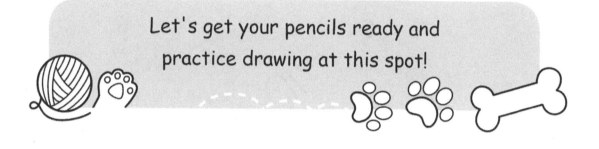

Garden Snail

1

2

3

4

5

6

7

8

9

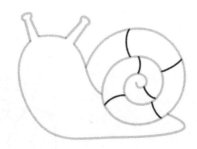

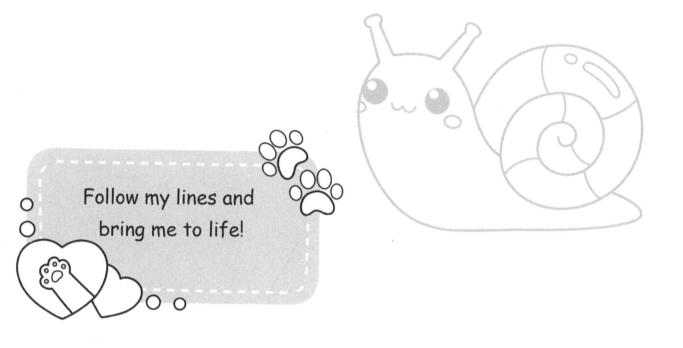

Follow my lines and bring me to life!

Ready, set, draw! Let's practice your skills right here and now!

Rabbit

1

2

3

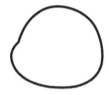

4

5

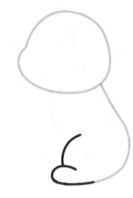

6

7

8

9

Trace my lines to
sharpen your skills.

It's time to show off our drawing skills!
Let's practice at this place!

Gerbil

Follow my outline for a tracing challenge.

Ready to have some fun and practice drawing?
Let's do it here!

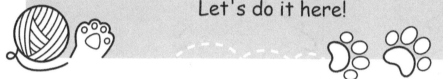

Hedgehog

1

2

3

4

5

6

7

8

9

Hone your skills with
a trace of me.

Get your pencils ready,
it's time to practice drawing here!

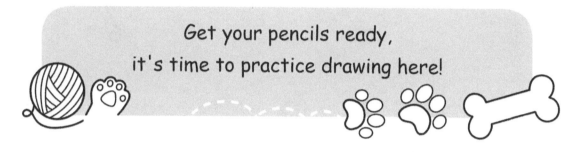

Angelfish

 1

 **2**

 3

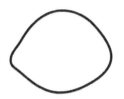

 4

 5

 6

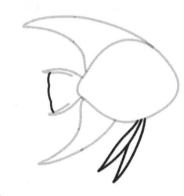

 7

 8

 9

Angelfish

Let me be your guide,
trace and improve.

Let's have some fun and practice
our drawing skills here!

Duck

Follow my lines and
bring me to life!

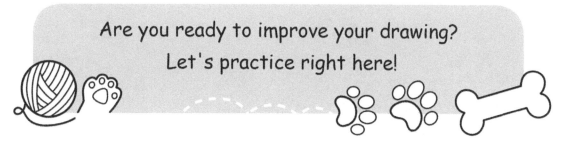

Are you ready to improve your drawing?
Let's practice right here!

Ferret

Trace my lines to sharpen your skills.

Let's use this space to practice our drawing and improve your skills!

Golden Retriever

 1
 2
 3

 4
 5
 6

7
8
9

Follow my outline for a tracing challenge.

Let's get your pencils ready and practice drawing at this spot!

Congratulations, budding artist!

You've officially unlocked a whole new level of artistic awesomeness by completing our incredible how-to-draw book! Give yourselves a round of "paws" and a cheer from your furry (or scaly) friends.

Now, you've got the power to transform any blank canvas into a pet paradise, where imagination meets wagging tails and purr-fect poses. Remember, the sky's the limit, so let your creativity "hop," "slither," and "fly" as you embark on countless artistic adventures. Keep those pencils sharp and continue spreading smiles with your fantastic drawings.

Fur-real, you're the next big thing in the art world!

Made in the USA
Las Vegas, NV
04 December 2024

13396986R00063